HER WILD WHISPERS

HER WILD WHISPERS

ORIGINAL POEMS AND GUIDED WRITING EXERCISES
WRITTEN BY BIANCA STOCKDEN TO INSPIRE CREATIVITY AND SELF-LOVE

FOR THE MOTHERS, THE TRANSFORMERS.
THE BUTTERFLIES

HER WILD
WHISPERS

THIS JOURNAL BELONGS TO

CONTENTS PAGE

The Poems, Prompts & Purpose.. I
Before we Begin.. III
Tips to Get You Started... IV

PART 1: POEMS & PROMPTS

Childhood

♡ Task 1- 'Shell Collecting'- Childhood memories................................. 3
♡ Task 2- 'Hey Little Girl'- A letter to your childhood self................... 6
♡ Task 3- 'My Mother Had a Mother'- Exploring family patterns........ 10
♡ Task 4- 'Your Masterpiece'- Inner child reflection............................. 14
♡ Task 5- 'The Love Around me Had Collapsed'- Our sad stories....... 18

Pregnancy Birth and Motherhood

♡ Task 1- 'Carving Your Way'- Pregnancy reflection............................. 23
♡ Task 2- 'Life Cycle'- Have we transformed? 27
♡ Task 3- 'Daily Gift'- Reflecting on your love for your children......... 30
♡ Task 4- 'Ocean'- Your birth story.. 33
♡ Task 5- 'Lessons in Love'- Lessons you've learnt in Motherhood..... 37
♡ Task 6- 'New Reflection'- The contradictions of Motherhood.......... 40
♡ Task 7- 'Sweet Everythings!'- Writing sweet everythings................. 43
♡ Task 8- 'My World'- Your words to them.. 46
♡ Task 9- 'Heart Pound'- Looking at the 'big picture'............................ 49
♡ Task 10- 'Support'- Your Motherhood vows....................................... 53

Self Development

♡ Task 1- 'Climb Rugged Mountains'- Writing a bucket list................. 57
♡ Task 2- 'Power'- Your superpowers... 60
♡ Task 3- 'Affirmation Armour'- Writing Affirmations........................ 63
♡ Task 4- 'Presence'- Exercising presence 67

♡Task 5- 'Best Friends With my Dark Side'- Sexy escapades............ 70
♡Task 6- 'Sweet Words'- Writing a love letter to you..................... 74
♡Task 7- 'Always Rising'- Future goals...................................... 78
♡Task 8- 'A Work of Art'- Body love.. 82
♡Task 9- 'Be'- Your identity... 85
♡Task 10- 'Harmony'- Self love.. 88
♡Task 11- 'Brave'- Your wins... 91
♡Task 12- 'A Deep Dive'- The hard bits..................................... 94
♡Task 13- 'Self Doubt'... 98
♡Task 14- 'Wildfires'- Gratitude 101
♡Task 15- 'Ripples'- Your life ripples....................................... 105
♡Task 16- 'Echoes'- Exploring 'women's' issues........................ 108

Relationships

♡Task 1- 'Spread The Love'- Writing love notes......................... 113
♡Task 2- 'Feast'- Healthy relationships.................................... 117
♡Task 3- 'Independence'- Your village..................................... 121
♡Task 4- 'Bond'- Your relationship with your mother................... 125
♡Task 5- 'Joy'- 'Blooming' mums... 129
♡Task 6- 'Thump'- Love work... 132
♡Task 7- 'She is Admirable'- Your female inspiration................... 136

PART 2- CREATIVE WRITING SPACE   140
General Journalling Ideas... 141
Writing a Haiku... 142
Writing a Ballad.. 143
Free Verse... 144

Acknowledgements.. 217
'Together in the Thick of Love'.. 218
A note from Bianca 219

♡*Colour the heart of any poems that resonate with you, for easy reference!*

THE POEMS, PROMPTS AND PURPOSE

Poems began to pour out of me like a weeping waterfall early into motherhood. They came during the sunshine and the raging storms. In the deep and dark of a lonely nursery and in the sweetest cuddles on the couch. Motherhood cracked me open in a way that I was not prepared for. It beamed a bright light on the feelings about myself that I never knew existed or ones that I had tried to bury away. But the beauty of motherhood has a way of exposing our feelings. Poetry is the expression of this.

It made me reflect on my own childhood and the influence that it has over me as a woman and a mother. Without laying blame, I have come to learn that I did not receive the love that I craved as a child. I did not have a 'bad' childhood and I had parents that loved me, but something did not make its way to my heart and as such I grew up with a longing for love. My parents gave me everything in their capacity and I am grateful for that.

Poetry has allowed me to organise my feelings and stories in a way that makes sense to me and has helped me unpack and still my overactive mind. Poetry is an expression of feelings. Most are simply just that. Few follow some structure.

Throughout this journal, there are 38 original poems and writing prompts. All mothers, new and experienced, are invited to explore the topics. Every stage of motherhood brings about a new set of challenges and invites us to explore different corners of ourselves. As such, it is suited to all mothers.

Each writing prompt begins with a poem. The poem is a springboard for personal reflection through a task or question. I hope that my openness and vulnerability encourages you to think deeply about your transformation into motherhood. I hope it helps you reflect on what fills you up and what triggers you, in the hope that you feel lighter, nurtured and closer to the version of yourself that you aspire to be.

May the words that you read and write help you see that you are enough. More than enough. Enough for yourself and for the ones that you love. May they help you grow wings that are inspired to fly free, exploring this big, beautiful, chaotic season of life.

BEFORE WE BEGIN

'Heard and Seen'

This is a reminder that you are not her
And she is not you
You are authentic and write your own story
The one in your heart that's true

Some carried babies in their bellies
Others in their hearts and hands
Some chose a path to parent alone
While others had a different plan

Some had babies that were a long time coming
But worth the anxious wait
Many rainbows didn't make it to Earth
Parents forced to accept that fate

Some never witnessed what a mother could be
Others had more than one
Some didn't choose this path at all
A past can not be undone

No matter the trail you've taken so far
Who you love or where you've been
Know that each and every day
You are loved and heard and seen

I see you and welcome all people to this journal. It is yours. I have written these poems through my own lens, but not yours. I invite you to see the tasks through your own light and adapt them to reflect your unique narrative.

You are important, valid and special. Welcome!

TIPS TO GET YOU STARTED

- Imagine these pages are a compassionate ear, loving unconditionally and craving your vulnerability.

- Remember that you are in control of your own narrative.

- Start. Just start. Pick up a pen and begin to write.

- Don't be afraid to make mistakes, add detail at another time, remove, or completely change your mind. You can always glue empty pages over the top of a response and start again. Just don't allow the fear of making a mistake rob you of the lightness you can feel by expressing yourself, right now.

- There are a collection of writing prompts throughout this journal. You are invited to complete them in any order you need. Some are lighthearted and some require deep reflection. They cover a range of topics so try to choose what you need, when you need it.

- Be kind to yourself. Just being here is brave.

PART ONE

POEMS AND GUIDED WRITING PROMPTS

CHILDHOOD

1. SHELL COLLECTING

A child collects memories like shells, placing
them in deep, ravenous and
unforgettable pockets

/   /

TASK 1 - CHILDHOOD MEMORIES

Write a list of happy memories you have as a child. Perhaps they were places you visited, people you spent time with or activities you participated in.

Take one memory and sketch a picture of the scene. Go on. Take a chance. No one is watching. Stick people count!

2. HEY LITTLE GIRL

Hey little girl,
Don't you worry
It's out of your hands
It's not your story

Hey little girl,
Put that down
Worry is too heavy
To carry around

Hey little girl,
Just be a child
With no care in the world
Run wild & smile

Hey little girl,
They love you
They may be distracted
But love, they do

Hey little girl,
She'll be ok
You can't keep worrying
That he won't stay

Hey little girl,
I see your big heart
You'll use this forever
Love is your art

Hey little girl,
I know your future
I know you'll be loved
As a wife and a mother

Hey little girl
Your future is bright
So throw away those fears
And all the self doubt

/ /

TASK 2 - DEAR ME...

Many of us feel like we were not provided with everything that we truly needed as a child. Some of us felt unloved or unseen, unheard, misunderstood or were riddled with self doubt and fear. Many of us did not feel like we were enough. This may have come from our family, community or the media.

Write a letter to your childhood self. Give her the advice that you wanted to hear. Reassure her. Acknowledge her. Love her.

3. MY MOTHER HAD A MOTHER

My mother had a mother
And another before that
They passed down all their stories
And the wisdom that they had

Running to the wild
Was a trait shared by many
A lust to see the world
Sent them on an endless journey

They felt a constant longing
For what? They didn't know
But the feeling seemed to travel
Travel through their bones

Strong wings were passed on
To those that came along
It cursed them of a feeling
Of one place they could belong

But here I am today
Working on an inner peace
To enjoy being present
Because right here is good for me

TASK 3 - FAMILY PATTERNS

What family traits do you see being passed down through generations? These could be ideals about raising a family, personality traits, or mental health patterns.

What do you wish to continue?

What would you like to end with you?

Are there some thoughts or actionable steps you can take to end any negative intergenerational patterns?

4. YOUR MASTERPIECE

The little girl you once were is threaded through you. She is woven through your thoughts and words and ways, entwining who you were with who you are. She helps you decide which patterns to repeat and which to repair. She is sewn into your roots. She is your masterpiece.

TASK 4 - INNER CHILD

Your 'inner child' is the culmination of your experiences and feelings from childhood. They often set your beliefs about yourself and how you interact with others.

What did you want more or less of as a child?

Can you see why and how that was not possible for caregivers to provide?

What do you wish you could tell your childhood self?

How have your childhood experiences (positive or negative) helped you be the mum that you aspire to be?

5. THE LOVE AROUND ME HAD COLLAPSED

The sun had not
yet seen one lap
When the love around
me had collapsed

Cries heard by
The watching moon
Were pouring out
of every room

Consumed by
Your broken heart
Loving must have
Felt quite hard

In my bed
I laid alone
Calling out with
Every moan

Please don't leave
My cry would say
I wasn't enough to
Make him stay

/ /

TASK 5 - OUR SAD STORIES

Not all of our memories of childhood are positive. Some people have experienced trauma, loss and neglect. Others witnessed family conflict, were the victims of bullying or grew up with complicated relationships or little self esteem.

To understand and face our stories allows us to work towards healing them. This takes courage and bravery. Lucky you have both.

Recall a sad event or feeling from childhood. Retell the events in as much or as little detail as you need.

What did you feel then?

What emotions are stirred up now by retelling the story?

Do you think this story or feeling helped you in any way? Are you stronger or more compassionate towards others?

Has it impacted your parenting?

What would you say to your childhood self if you could go back to this situation?

PREGNANCY, BIRTH AND MOTHERHOOD

1. CARVING YOUR WAY

I clutch at my blooming belly. I am in awe of the female form even as I sit in the midst of it. Your magic makes me glow as every cell of us moves, bends, stretches and grows. You're carving your way into my body before you carve your way in the world.

Forever imprinted in me.

/   /

TASK 1 - PREGNANCY REFLECTION

We all experience pregnancy in such varied ways and it can differ from first to consecutive pregnancies too.

How did you find pregnancy? Was it a 'job' for you? Were you perpetually anxious about what could go wrong? Did you enjoy the flutters and flaunting of your bump?
Was it a journey to get to this point?
Did you have scares and complications along the way?
Which scan did you enjoy most?
What advice would you give to newly pregnant women?

Perhaps you carried your baby in your arms and not your belly. Explore your journey from the moment it all began. The decision, the process, the highs and lows. The excitement and nervousness,

Use these questions as a guide to write your own reflection.

2. LIFE CYCLE

Unravelling the cocoon. Child. Woman. Mother. When did we transform? Transcend? With your first heartbeat or your first breath? The irreversible change etched in my web.

-the life cycle of a mother

TASK 2 - HAVE WE TRANSFORMED?

Do you agree with the sentiment that now you are a mother you have 'transformed'? That you are a different person? Have you 'lost' the woman that you were prior to motherhood or does she still exist?

Free write about your thoughts and opinions on this!

3. DAILY GIFT

When I think I can't love you more
The sun rises and I'm more in awe

/   /

TASK 3 - A LOVE LIKE NO OTHER

Is there really a love greater than the one you feel for your children? Did it surprise you? Does it continue to grow?

Express your thoughts and love below:

4. OCEAN

Guided by your inner rhythm which sends pulses through your bare body. Some ripples and others raging waves sending you out of your depth and back above the surface. Again and again. Waves rolling in and rolling out. Breath in, breath out. Your mind chasing your body. Your body which has taken over like it's been told what to do by the women before you. Peaks of strength with troughs of pain. Peaks of control with troughs of surrender. Peaks of magic with troughs of instinct.

An ocean of love is born.

/ /

TASK 4 - YOUR BIRTH STORY

Retell your birth story/ies in the form of your choosing. Perhaps you'd like to experiment with a poem or maybe you'd rather write a recount or simply use dot points.

You get to take ownership of your story. Write the moments and feelings you want to remember in your bones. Don't shy away from the pain, discomfort or fear, but own it.

*Perhaps you did not give birth. Explore how your baby came into the world and into your loving arms.

Your story to tell:

5. LESSONS LEARNT IN LOVE

I bottle up the love I crave
And pour it into you
Your heart is full when mine is not
But that's how I get through

I thought I didn't have enough
But you taught me something new
You taught me love does not run out
My heart, it grew with you

I've learnt Love shall not be stored
Free flowing we shall choose
Your being saved me from myself
My mind and heart renewed

TASK 5 - LESSONS YOU'VE LEARNT

Every day you are learning about this new little human and what it takes to raise children. There are lessons at every age and stage. Parenting has a way of challenging what you thought about the world and opening up a new perspective. Being a mum for me, made me realise that I have such a realm of influence over the little humans that I spend my time with. A daunting and enormous privilege.

What lessons have you learnt about yourself and the world?

6. NEW REFLECTION

A reflection I barely recognise, lost in a disguise. New scenes that fill my tired eyes cascading in loving cries. A new beginning I've come to realise, was sent with your sunrise. Every action and breath I improvise, creating brand new highs. Energised, I realise, this is life's best surprise.
-Motherhood

TASK 6 - THE CONTRADICTIONS

It is a surprise. A shock. An irreversible one. There is good, bad and ugly, all at once and often about the same thing. Motherhood is full of contradictions and pulling of the heart from one extreme to the other.

- I'm tired, but lay in bed looking at photos of you
- I need space. But miss you when you're not in my arms
- I struggle with the appearance of my body. But love that it feeds you

What other contradictions do you feel?

7. SWEET EVERYTHINGS!

You are sunshine, rainbows, waves and more.
The most precious thing I love and adore

***

When I think I can't love you more
The sun rises and I'm more in awe

***

I see the sun shine through your eyes
Its warmth you radiate
You set sweet light upon the earth
With joy that you create

/ /

TASK 7 - WRITING SWEET EVERYTHINGS !

Words of love and appreciation spoken to our children helps them create a sense of worth and belonging.

Create your own sweet verses that you can repeat to your babes regularly. Make them rhyme... or don't!

8. MY WORLD

My baby, I miss you
When it's only been a moment
I want to hold you tight
When you need your space to grow
I want to share your every sight
But I want you to explore
I want to heal your every hurt
But I need you to be brave

I want to tell you, you're my world
But that's too much to know

/ /

TASK 8 - YOUR WORDS TO THEM

What do you always want your children to know? They are loved and worthy? What do they mean to you? How do you want them to feel?

Prepare a brief speech you could give to them:

9. HEART POUND

As another day turns away from the sun, were you everything you hoped to be?
Did you shout your story with bellows and whistles and bold whispers?
Did you stand on the precarious edge of it all while creating a vastness of space?
Did your heart pound profusely for what matters most?
Because that's what matters most.
Did it light a fire inside you as big as the fire that made you?
As big as the one we chase each night?

Run to the sunrise, rise, restart.

/ /

TASK 9 - THE BIG PICTURE

The Big Picture. What do you value most above all else? I bet it is not how much awake time your children have or if granny gives them that extra sugary biscuit or if a nap gets cut short for whatever reason. What do you want most for your children? The big picture stuff. It is so easy to get caught up in worrying about the little things and trying to create the most rigid routines and rules but sometimes we need to take a step back and look on with a broader perspective.

What do you value above all else? What do you want most for your children?

Does this change your perspective on some of the smaller challenges?

10. SUPPORT

I will support you. Not in the hand holding kind of way but the stand back and watch you soar and carry you if you need, kind of way.

I will hear you. And not in the listening kind of way but the delving into those words to find your truth, kind of way.

I will see you. And not in the looking kind of way but the searching into your soul, to learn who you truly are, kind of way.

I will love you. Not in the heart fluttering kind of way but the unconditional, selfless, with every cell of my body, kind of way.

For always.

TASK 10 - MOTHERHOOD VOWS

Ooof this is a big job! We have so much responsibility to create healthy and emotionally stable children. We may or may not succeed but we can try. Let's break it down...

What are your promises to your children? They can be as simple or as grand as you with them to be.

SELF DEVELOPMENT

1. CLIMB RUGGED MOUNTAINS

Dance with the flowers
Sing to the sun
Climb rugged mountains
Until the day's done

/ /

TASK 1 - A BUCKET LIST

Life isn't over.

Life has not begun.

Life is simply being lived.

You have so many years ahead of you, with and without children. What 'rugged mountains' do you still want to climb?

Write a 'bucket list' of all of the places you want to visit and activities you want to do and dreams you want to fulfil.

Dream big!

2. POWER

Electric pulses run through your body, emitting and attracting love and light.

Woman, you are powerful.

/ /

TASK 2 - YOUR SUPERPOWERS

Heck lady, you keep little humans alive! You are amazing. What else are you proud of? Motherhood related and not!

Write a list of all of your life's superpowers and achievements!

3. AFFIRMATION ARMOUR

I capture words one by one
And throw them to the ground
Like captives inside my head
Thoughts scream and thrash around

I stand up strong and try to fight
But they take over control
Taking all the light I made
While trying to heal my soul

I repeat kind words I know are true
Over and over again
And just like that, they are gone
My mind begins to mend

TASK 3 - WRITING AFFIRMATIONS

Unfortunately we are all victims of negative self talk at times during our lives. Motherhood can be a particular time of self doubt, anxiety and loneliness, our harshest critics being ourselves.

You need some 'affirmation armour'. These are 'I' statements that you need to write when feeling positive and strong. These affirmations should be repeated regularly (daily and in the mirror) to encourage a positive mindset that can help you break free of the negativity when it comes to visit.

I am kind to myself
I am doing an amazing job
I am a selfless mother
I nourish myself and my family
I embrace this season
I believe in myself and my ability

Your affirmations:

4. PRESENCE

Your heart matches the beat of the earth. The sea propels your blood. Swaying trees, the rhythm of your breath. The sun warms your skin.

-presence

/ /

TASK 4 - PRESENCE

Make yourself a cup of tea and take yourself to a quiet place.

Ground your feet on the floor. Take a deep belly breath and exhale it through your mouth with an audible sigh. Repeat that inhale and loud exhale a few times.

Place your hand on your heart and feel its beat. Close your mouth and breathe deeply. You are alive and living in this very moment.

What can you see?

Hear?

Feel?

Smell?

List any words that come to mind:

Capture this moment. Sketch a picture of what you see or how you feel. There is joy in the vulnerability of attempting something that feels uncomfortable. There is also so much beauty around you, if you allow yourself a moment to see it.

5. BEST FRIENDS WITH MY DARK SIDE

I'm best friends with my dark side
She's fierce and sexy and strong
She's all bad kinds of good
And all the right parts of wrong

She sends me to my depths
Lights fires in my core
Gets hearts and fingers moving
Makes me explore a little more

She sends me to new heights
Cracks open all my fears
Makes me grasp and tackle all of them
Until they disappear

I'm best friends with my dark side
She's fierce and sexy and strong
My deepest, darkest secret
In my shadows all along

TASK 5 - SEXY ESCAPADES

Maybe for you it's right now or maybe it feels like you will never be her again, but at some point soon you will be ready to be that carefree, non boob leaking, healed stitches, sexy version of yourself ready to get down and go down. So let's get ready and raunchy.

Think Literotica. Describe a sexual fantasy that you can't wait to live out. Spare no detail. Describe the setting, the outfits, the leading sexts, the conversations, the way clothes are removed and body parts are entangled. Unleash your sexual goddess. If a narrative is not for you, record your 'must dos' as dot points!

Your sexual fantasy!:

6. SWEET WORDS

Say sweet words which spring from your lips to mine
and back.
Over and over.

TASK 6 - LOVE LETTER TO YOU

You've come so far. What do you love about yourself? What are you proud of? What challenges have you overcome? What has surprised you about what you can handle and overcome?

Write yourself a love letter!

7. ALWAYS RISING

Don't chase the sweet days that have tiptoed off the horizon. Instead, marvel at what you can make tomorrow with your collection of beautiful yesterdays. Sweeter days keep rising.

/ /

TASK 7 - FUTURE GOALS

We can sit and be sad that our babies are growing too quickly and that 'time is a thief' or we could marvel in what we have done and created thus far and build on it for an even more amazing future. We have so much more to achieve and look forward to.

What does life (family, home, career, health) look like for you in...

1 year:

5 years:

10 years:

8. A WORK OF ART

She is a body of work
A work of art
She is lines and shapes that point to the stars, pull on the moon, circle the sun and tiptoe over the dunes, dancing her way home... to you

She is honest and forgiving, heart and soul.
She's a painting of your story
Every rise and fall

She is contours and colours, skin and bone. She is rough and smooth.

A shield of your own

So love her

/   /

TASK 8 - BODY LOVE

There is no doubt that growing, birthing and raising babies changes your body. This can be an adjustment and take some specific self love to feel good about. Combined with being tired, the sharing of your body in physical ways like breastfeeding, and often having less time to be active, you may not be giving the love to your body that it truly deserves.

This exercise is about honouring what your body can do, what it has done for you and all that you love about it. She is your vessel and she deserves love and recognition. Tell her.

Label the bits you love (or trying to) and what they have done for you and your children.

Eg. I love my heart for loving you. I love my skin for being a comforting place for you to nestle….

9. BE

In a world that wants to know what you are- Be a sun seeker, a love maker, a bird chaser, a rain dancer, a mountain climber, a story teller, a letter writer, a wave rider.

In copious amounts.

TASK 9 - YOUR IDENTITY

Who are you? What are the characteristics and roles that you want to be known for? What are your key personality traits? What do you care about? Who do you care about? What sets your soul on fire? Perhaps this has changed recently or perhaps you are solid on this.

Write your own bio.

10. HARMONY

Harmony in my own company. A melodic chime building and falling in sweet song. The sound of peace and self love filling my ears and eyes and all the spaces that have been quiet.

/   /

TASK 10 - SELF LOVE

When was a time where you felt at complete ease with yourself, confident and totally in love with you?

How do you show yourself love and practise self care?

Set 3 intentions to implement in the next 3 weeks to encourage some more self love. (Perhaps it is right now, taking time to honour and connect with yourself through journalling)

11. BRAVE

You my sister are brave. Brave like a blooming flower baring itself to the sun. Digging your roots into the earth, claiming your rightful space. Growing. Growing thorns along with fruit and beauty.

/ /

TASK 11 - YOUR WINS

Make a list of your motherhood wins so far. Big and small. There is plenty of room. This one is to revisit!

12. A DEEP DIVE

Diving to the depths
In search of a breath.
Gasp

/ /

TASK 12 - THE HARD BITS

It sometimes takes hitting rock bottom before we are able to find the right path and finally take a breath and gain perspective. Think about an event or period of parenting that you have found particularly challenging. It could have been a particularly low time for you or a battle that took some time to move through.

Describe a challenge you've faced

How did you feel when you had 'dived to the depths'?

Did you make it out? How and who helped you to do that?

What can you put in place to try to avoid going to that deep, dark place again?

13. SELF DOUBT

I'm confident I'm unsure
I'm unsure I'm confident
-the crippling self doubt of a capable woman

TASK 13 - SELF DOUBT

Seriously, none of us know what we are doing! It is a learning curve at every moment and stage. It is often the smart, independent and capable women who struggle with the unknown so much. They have been used to working towards and achieving goals their entire life and then all of a sudden, this thing that they want to 'succeed' at, decides to live outside of what they've read and researched. There is a constant battle between, 'I've got this' and 'I don't have this at all' and so the self doubt creeps in and lingers far beyond its welcome.

Has this been true for you?

Is it a struggle to feel a lack of confidence? Why do you think we like to feel like 'experts' at all we do?

What specific doubts have you had?

14. WILDFIRES

It's the habitual that sets my heart on fire
It's you who sends wildfires through my entire body

Flames in my veins

TASK 14 - GRATITIDE

/ /

What are the bits of your everyday life that you love and appreciate? The routines? The people? What is it about the place you live in?

What are you grateful for?

15. RIPPLES

Don't let those toes tiptoe anywhere.
Stamp and stomp.
Tear up the floor beneath you
Make the earth rumble and shake and vibrate

Then twirl and spin and love along the ripples that you make.

TASK 15 - YOUR RIPPLES

How do you want to be remembered as a woman? What impact do you want to make on this world?

What ripples will you create?

16. ECHOES

Women are climbing mountains
Demanding to be seen
I'm waiting in the valley
Wondering where I want to be

They're shouting to the wind
Of causes they hold dear
For bodies and climate and rights
So many things to fear

I listen to the echoes
That swirl around my mind
Searching for my fight
Of which I want to find

These women I admire
For their courage and their voice
I will shout with them
LET OUR BODIES, BE OUR CHOICE

/ /

TASK 16 - EXPLORING WOMEN'S ISSUES

There are so many frightening issues that affect us as women directly. These same issues might affect our children in the future.

What inspires you about the women you know, the ones in your community and the ones experiencing hardship around the world?

Is there a social, political or environmental issue that you are particularly concerned about?

What emotions are sparked within you?

Is there any part of this issue that you can control or can take action on?

Say It!

What words would you write on your banner in a protest for this issue?

RELATIONSHIPS

1. SPREAD THE LOVE

Swap sticks and stones for love notes
and the world will flood with love
Put them in your pockets
or spread the love to everyone

/ /

TASK 1 - LOVE NOTES

Who do you want to send love notes to? We don't verbalise our gratitude and love to those we treasure, enough.

Tell the ones you love that you love them and why. Maybe you want to thank them for their support during your journey into motherhood?

Let's write some love notes...

2. FEAST

You feasted on my sweet and plentiful heart in the only way I knew that love did. With yours already devoured, you tried to fill it with mine. We were both so hungry for love that we brushed together the scraps until they had all disappeared, leaving nothing but a destructive trail.
-unhealthy love

TASK 2 - HEALTHY RELATIONSHIPS

The unhealthy relationships and heartbreak that we experience can be the lessons we learn in what we deserve and what a healthy relationship looks like.

*You choose which relationship/s you want to explore. These may or may not be the romantic type.

What makes a relationship 'healthy'?

Do you believe your relationship encompasses these attributes? We can always make improvements. What are some goals you could implement into your relationship to help it thrive in this challenging season?

What do you hope for your children's future relationships?

3. INDEPENDENCE

I want to burden those
who would not feel burdened.
Instead, I burden myself
by drowning in independence.

TASK 3 - YOUR VILLAGE

You can not do this alone. We were never meant to be mothers in isolation. But sadly, that is how many of us are living in our modern world. Sometimes you can feel so alone, but you are not. Let's explore your village!

Write the names of people who fit the description of each section of the circle on the following page.

1- Your ride or die. No detail spared. Would call in the middle of the night

2- The people in your active WhatsApp group. You often overshare with them. Happy to ask for and receive advice from

3- The people you want to go on coffee and chat dates with. Surface-level sleep routine chat but won't tell them how many times you've cried this week

4- The 'Boundary Riders'- the people who you are close with but need to set some clear boundaries for

Your Village:

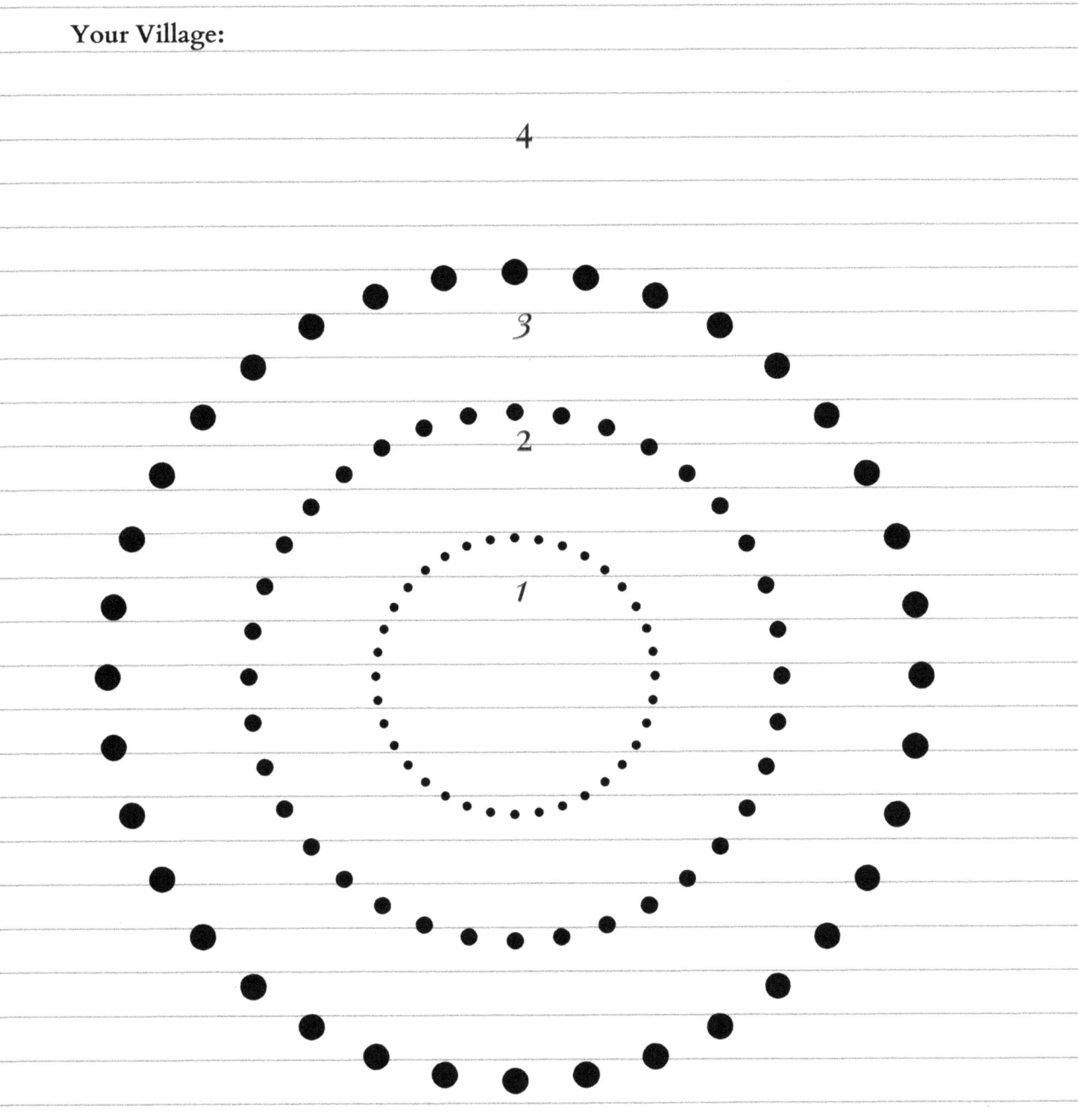

Boundaries:

Who do you need to set some boundaries with? What could this look like?

4. BOND

Mother and child.
The strongest, most fickle bond.

TASK 4 - YOUR RELATIONSHIP WITH YOUR MOTHER

Becoming a mum, naturally. makes you reflect on your own relationship with your parents, how they have influenced you and what attributes you admire (or despise). We are all complex beings, our parents are not exempt!

Describe your own relationship with your mother (*or other care giver)

Brainstorm it!

Brainstorm it!

How would you like to be described as a mother?

5. JOY

Joy is honouring the blooming flowers that surround you, not being blinded by the ones in your imagination.

TASK 5 - BLOOMING MUMS

/ /

Who are some 'blooming' mums that you are inspired by? These are the ones that you think are "killing it" (coping with the ups and downs). What makes you see them as a 'good' mum? How do they cope with the hard bits? What can you learn from them?

Blooming Mum 1:

Blooming Mum 2:

Blooming Mum 3:

Blooming Mum 4:

6. THUMP

Don't you see what I see? Feel how I feel? Don't you long for love like I do?
Does your heart not crave more like mine does?
Clenched in patience, paused in anticipation.

Thump (says the heart).
Here it comes (in troves).

      Love is on its way…

TASK 6 - LOVE WORK

It is often the relationship that doesn't get the same attention it once did. The one with your partner, the one that came first. There is sleep deprivation, changing lives, roles and routines which add tension (a little or a lot!) to what was once a solid relationship. It can be difficult to avoid feeling resentment when it feels like it is the mother who makes many of the big changes to her life.

*Life can cause all relationships to change and they are all worth working on. Adapt this task to suit your personal situation. Perhaps choose your closest support person or friend.

What are some positive words can you use to describe your partner? Why did you fall in love with them?

Make a list of actions they have performed that have made you feel seen, valued and loved.

How has their life had to adjust in this season? What challenges might they be facing?

What are 3 things you can implement to work on this relationship (acknowledge, have a difficult conversation, plan a phone free couch date etc.)?

7. SHE IS ADMIRABLE

Women are driven.
Driven to the edge. Driven to the ground. Driven to rise.
Driven to dare. Driven to fight. Driven to speak. Driven to sing. Driven to evolve. Driven to soar.

Driven to dance among the stars.

/   /

TASK 7 - YOUR FEMALE INSPIRATION

Who is one woman you admire? They may or may not be a mother and you may or may not have even met them. We draw inspiration from the women around us and those who we see as amazing. They help us to forge our own paths, perhaps in some likeness to them.

Who do you admire?

Age:

Family status:

Positive traits:

Do they have any 'faults' that you know of?

What do you admire about them?

Can you see yourself in their image?

What are 3 questions you'd ask them over dinner if you had the chance?

PART TWO

CREATIVE WRITING SPACE

GENERAL JOURNALLING IDEAS

- What makes you proud?
- What are you are grateful for?
- Describe an emotion that you are feeling;
    - What is the emotion?
    - Is it helpful to you right now?
    - Where do you think it comes from?
    - Can you think of ways to encourage (positive emotion) or discourage (negative) the feeling?
- Write a list of recent positive experiences
- Write a list of people in your life that you adore and the reason why
- What is your greatest adventure?
- What is the best advice that you have received? Who would you like to pass that advice onto?

- How about trying some poetry! See the following pages for some guidelines!

WRITING A HAIKU

- A Haiku is a traditional Japanese form of poetry which follows a specific and simple structure
- They are 3 lines long
- They are usually about nature but can be adapted to represent whatever you like!
- 5 syllables in the first line, 7 in the second and 5 in the third

Examples:

Spread your wings lady
There is beauty to be seen
If you let yourself

You shine like the Sun
And spread those beams to your loves
Soak in all their light

'I am your mother'
The sweetest words I've spoken
Can you hear the love?

Your turn!

WRITING A BALLAD

- A Ballad is a form of poetry which usually tells a story
- There are 4 lines in each verse
- The second and fourth lines in each verse, rhyme.
- A ballad attempts to have a song like rhythm where the first and third lines contain four beats and the second and fourth lines contain three beats. (I don't always achieve this but that is the joy with creative licence right?!')

Example:

The Ground Beneath You

The ground was placed beneath you
For your little feet to travel
You've been gifted to this wild world
Its mystery you'll unravel

The sky was placed above you
For your wings to explore
You've been gifted to this wild world
Oh baby you will soar

The sea was placed beside you
To dive in deep below
You've been gifted to this wild world
Grow, baby grow

The stars were placed above you
To guide you on your way
You've been gifted to this wild world
To shine every day

The sun was sent to warm you
To light up what you see
You've been gifted to this wild world
To be who you want to be

Additional Examples: 'Heard & Seen' pg. III
'Best Friends With my Dark Side' pg. 70
'Together in the Thick of Love' pg. 218

Your turn!

FREE VERSE

- They follow no specific rules or patterns
- They can still rhyme and have a set rhythm, if you choose
- Select a topic that interests you and that evokes lots of emotion
- Use your senses and brainstorm words and phrases that come to mind
- Experiment with figurative language

Example:

Alone has a new feeling
An indulgence trapped in missing you.
Locked up in the thoughts of you that I have not let go of.
When alone passes I will want it back. But here I am writing about you when I am desperately seeking solitude.

***

Sometimes the words flood from the sky and other times it is in the stillness that a whisper comes to walk on the paper. Circles and lines that make patterns, telling a story that I never knew was there.

Your turn!

ACKNOWLEDGEMENTS

Thank you to all of the incredible, generous, honest and selfless women that I get to 'mum' with. You have been there as a listening ear, as a voice of reason, a distraction and as a teacher. Your strength and resilience has been truly inspiring to me.

Motherhood has made me appreciate how amazing women are, across the world and in every shape, form and role that they play.

To the women that I have known since we were on the cusp, somewhere between child/teen/adult, watching you become a mum and witnessing your children become their own people, is magic. Seeing a glimpse of your reflection in them, excites me for what they will do and who they will become.

To my big sister, my best friend. Thank you for being the open, vulnerable, bad-ass bitch that you are. Your friendship and support is my greatest treasure.

To my husband, thank you for riding this rollercoaster with me. You bring me down to Earth while letting me spread my wings. You are a generous and loving person, and I love parenting with you.

To my family and friends that have supported and encouraged me in life and with this project, thank you.

A POEM DEDICATED TO MY VERY OWN LADY LOVES

TOGETHER IN THE THICK OF LOVE

I want to have answers for all of your questions
But they are my questions too
I want you to know you are more than enough
You wish I knew it too

I think of you awake in the middle of the night
While I'm doing the same
Kissing precious heads and filling hungry bellies
It's the love that keeps us sane

Here we are in the thick of the love
The hard, the fun, the new
You make this season a whole lot better
I'm so grateful to be doing it with you

I've known you for many spins of the moon
In a world long before this
But it's today we will treasure and want to repeat
These are the moments we'll miss

I don't say it often or maybe at all
But I'm immensely proud of you
You don't say the words but I think its true
That you feel it too

A NOTE FROM
BIANCA

Up until now, I have never thought I've been good at anything specific and that has really been something I've ruminated on. I am not defined by a hobby or skill (not from a lack of trying a million new hobbies regularly). Now, I am much more sure of who I am rather than what I do. I am kind, creative, active and all embracing. My life revolves around satisfying those personal qualities. I believe my purpose is to help others feel good about themselves. This is why I am here. Motherhood can be a time of self doubt, loneliness, questioning of identity and fear of the unknown. I hope that I can help other mothers feel less alone and more able to cope with what is happening for them.

I am Bianca, 34 living on Whadjuk Noongar Boodjar, near the coast in Perth. I am married to Glenn and together we dream of the countries we want to travel to, with and without children. I am an adoring mum to my two year old boy who delights and challenges me in every moment. At the time of creating this book, a new life is growing inside me too. I am thrilled to see the growth of my two 'projects'; the baby and this journal!

Prior to becoming a mother, I worked as a primary school teacher. My favourite moments were working and visiting our remote communities and encouraging students to question their world, accept all people and relate to others with compassion.

I am obsessed with my beautiful home that makes me feel like I am wrapped in a giant hug whenever I'm in it. My safe and cosy place. Visits to the beach and sunny holidays with my friends and family are what I love most.

My mental health is a constant work in progress. I have tried (and will continue to try) mediation! I see a psychologist every now and then, prioritise a healthy lifestyle and have tried alternatives therapies like breath work. The one strategy that works best for me, is journalling. I enjoy formulating my messy thoughts into organised sentences that help me make sense of my world. Perhaps you will too.

So that is me and that is why.

I hope this book gives you wings to fly.

www.ingramcontent.com/pod-product-compliance
Lightning Source LLC
Chambersburg PA
CBHW061137010526
44107CB00069B/2967